THE
DEADLY
DIAMOND

First published 2025 by
FREMANTLE PRESS

Fremantle Press Inc. trading as Fremantle Press
PO Box 158, North Fremantle, Western Australia, 6159
fremantlepress.com.au



Designed by Dani Lurie, Balloon Dog Studio, balloondog.studio
Printed by Everbest Printing Investment Limited, China

A catalogue record for this book is available from the National Library of Australia

ISBN 9781760995058 (paperback)
ISBN 9781760995065 (ebook)

Fremantle Press is supported by the State Government through the Department of Local Government, Sport and Cultural Industries.

Fremantle Press respectfully acknowledges the Whadjuk people of the Noongar nation as the Traditional Owners and Custodians of the land where we work in Walyalup.

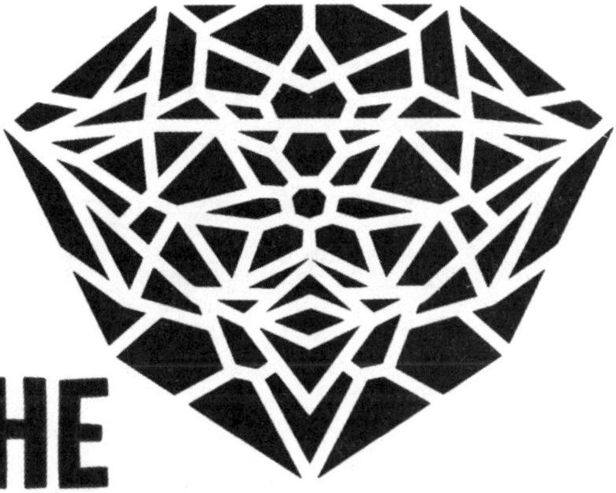

# THE DEADLY DIAMOND

MARK GREENWOOD
HISTORY HUNTER

*For Frané*

# INTRODUCTION

Armed guards stand at the entrance to a high-security chamber where a bewitching blue gem rotates in its bulletproof vault. Cold as ice, with a flash of fire, round and round it goes, pulsing with energy, shrouded in mystery.

Every year, millions of visitors from across the world climb the steps of the Smithsonian National Museum of Natural History in Washington, DC. They cross the polished stone floor and enter the Hall of Geology, Gems and Minerals. They've come to gaze upon the world's most notorious diamond.

The Hope Diamond is a miracle of nature, described as a 'fragment of midnight sky … still aglow

*The Hope Diamond.*

Photo © Chip Clark, Smithsonian National Museum of Natural History.

with star gleam'. But the deadly diamond is more famous for its bloodstained history than for its rarity. To be in its presence leaves no one unmoved.

Over the centuries, the legendary jewel has crossed oceans and continents, passing from thieves to commoners, kings and queens. It has been a symbol of love, of wealth and of power. It has been squabbled over, stolen, sold, resold, cut and recut. Many who have possessed it have squandered vast fortunes. Others have lost their lives. Some say it's cursed.

'Diamond' is derived from the Greek word *adamas*, meaning unconquerable or indestructable. Nature's precious creations have a mystique that sets them apart from all other gemstones. Over thousands of years, diamonds have been talismanic symbols of power worn in ornaments by nobility and military leaders, mounted in rings and pendants, bracelets and brooches to protect the wearer. They've adorned bejewelled thrones, sceptres and crowns reserved for royalty.

In mythology, diamonds have been attributed with potent energies that can take those who wear them to great heights or send possessors to their doom. Hauntings, creepy histories and superstitions are often associated with the world's most famous diamonds. For those with a taste for the sensational, storied diamonds outrank the curse of the tomb of Tutankhamun. Ever since nature's treasures were dug from dirt, humankind conjured a curious lore of precious stones and assigned special significance to diamonds.

Of all diamonds, the Hope Diamond's history is the most intriguing. Discovered in India, it is the largest known blue diamond. Though its shape is unsymmetrical, the Hope's colour and prismatic fire makes it one of the most stunning gemstones in the world. And according to legend, sinister forces lurk beneath its indigo surface.

The Hope Diamond's potency for bad luck is said to have its origins in an ancient curse. But can material objects, like diamonds, possess power or leave behind a trail of misfortune? Are the dark meanings bestowed on ancient artifacts simply superstitions imagined by humans? Or is the legendary curse associated with the famous blue diamond real?

To untangle myth from fact, join me on a journey back in time, where we leave the realm of superstition and enter that of history. To trace a diamond's remarkable life, we begin this History Hunter case file over one billion years ago.

# NATURE'S MIRACLE

No one knows the Hope Diamond's exact age other than to agree that it was conceived between one and three billion years ago. Its life began deep in the earth's mantle, one hundred and fifty kilometers below the planet's surface. Under intense heat and pressure, carbon atoms were compressed into the crystalised structure of a diamond — the hardest naturally occurring substance on earth.

After surviving birth in the firey throat of a volcano, and the violent eruption that brought it to the earth's surface in molten magma, the diamond came to rest on the Deccan Plateau in India. For millions of years, it remained entombed in solidified rock, tossed and tumbled in rivers of primeval slime that flowed from a ring of lofty mountains. Over time, the weathered rock casing eroded, freeing the diamond. In the sickle

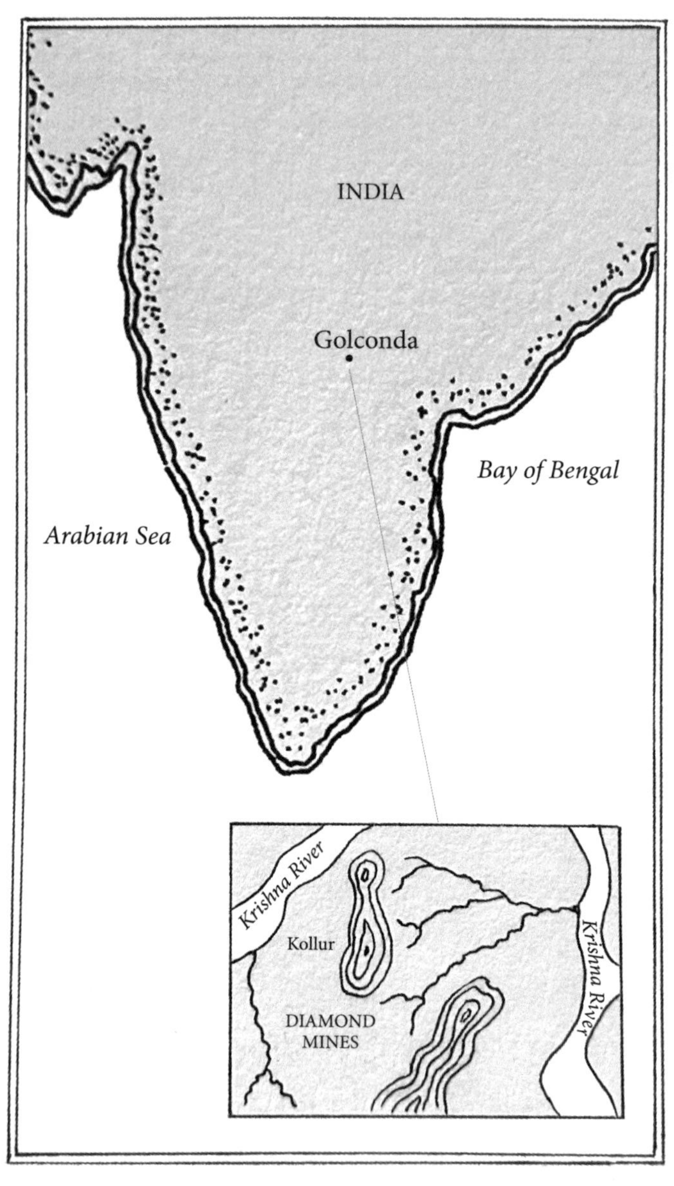


*Golconda and the Kollur mine
where the blue diamond was found.*

bend of the Krishna River, nature's miracle lay buried in the dirt.

Today, diamonds are mined in countries worldwide — from the frozen Siberian mines in Russia and the barren subarctic regions of Canada to the mountains and rivers of Africa. But between the sixteenth and early eighteenth centuries, the world's entire supply of diamonds came from India, where precious stones were sourced from the rich alluvial deposits of Golconda.

Many of the world's most famous diamonds were discovered at the Kollur mine on the bank of the Krishna River, where thousands of men, women and children worked in snake-infested conditions. Kollur, and a nearby cluster of mines, sustained the Golconda kingdom for three centuries.

In antiquity, the beauty and unequalled hardness of diamonds were sufficient reasons for the stones to become a source of value and trade. It was also said that diamonds possessed powers that could shield the wearer from danger. Mounted in amulets, they offered protection against bad luck and natural disasters. Diamonds were a symbol of strength and purity.

Some diamonds achieved mystical status based on religious beliefs, superstitions and the notion of invincibility. In ancient India, Vishnu, god of the heavens, governed all crystals, whatever their form or colour. White diamonds with eight crystal faces, were associated with Indra, the god of storms, thunder and lightning. The king, emperor or mogul could wear any colour, as he was lord of all castes. Brahmins, members of the priestly caste, could possess white or colourless diamonds. Yellow diamonds were for merchants and landowners. Warriors chose red diamonds. Dark grey diamonds were reserved for artisans and labourers. But of all the colours, blue was the most desirable.

Throughout the Middle Ages, extraordinary tales of a 'Valley of Diamonds' reached far beyond India to China, Arabia and Persia, before spreading to Europe. Books such as *One Thousand and One Nights*, *Sinbad the Sailor* and *The Travels of Marco Polo* described the strange lands where prized gems were found.

Later texts described sacred temple idols with eyes fashioned from enormous diamonds.

The diamonds that came from the fabled mines of Golconda were highly valued. Local rulers jealously guarded the source and kept the largest diamonds for themselves. The radiance of these diamonds was legendary. Many believed they contained a supernatural force. Prized for colour, clarity, size and beauty, some were pure as a drop of dew. Others were orange or apricot, red or apple-green, canary-yellow or pale-rose-pink. But the rarest colour of all was midnight-blue.

An enormous blue diamond was said to have been worshipped as the all-seeing eye of a temple idol. One night a crowd gathered, drawn by the wailing of the Brahmin priests. A great sacrilege had occurred. A wicked thief had plucked the coveted gem from the eye of the sacred idol. A sorrowful chant was uttered, casting a curse forevermore on any mortal who possessed the idol's eye.

That legendary blue diamond and the curse placed

on it continues to attract debate to this day. Was the blue diamond, known today as the Hope Diamond, stolen from the eye of an idol? Could a haunting aura of bad luck follow the diamond, casting a sinister spell from one owner to the next?

# VALLEY OF THE DIAMONDS

Jean-Baptiste Tavernier was a dreamer. He grew up in seventeenth-century France with tales of exotic people and places. His father was a map maker and Jean-Baptiste's desire to sample the charms of foreign lands was fuelled by the world described on his father's maps.

Four centuries ago, Tavernier embarked on six voyages over land and sea to the Far East — India, Ceylon and Persia. Along the way, he narrowly escaped the carnage of war, shipwreck and being chased by cutthroat pirates. He survived drowning, scandals, treachery and threats of assassination.

Tavernier developed an eye for objects of exquisite beauty. He looked for opportunities and learned the lessons of profit. He sought out luxurious curiosities, the finest pearls, royal-blue sapphires and blood-red rubies. He searched for jewels to feed the growing European desire for fine gemstones. During his voyages, Tavernier acquired a thorough knowledge of many languages and amassed a considerable fortune. He was feted by cardinals, politicians and prime ministers. He negotiated with kings and queens, emperors and moguls.

In 1663, the distinguished traveller embarked on his final voyage — an epic journey to the fortified city of Golconda that he'd seen on his father's maps. The article of trade to which he was solely devoted was the purchase of large diamonds of exceptional purity and luminosity.

From sunrise to sunset, Tavernier's nostrils filled with dust as his ox-drawn cavalcade creaked eastward along the ancient trade route. He passed through cities coated with grit and grime. On his journey to the fabled mines, where rivers washed dazzling treasures from their hiding places, he was greeted by cymbals, drums and costumed dancers. Temples with idols adorned with precious stones dotted the landscape.

In the 1600s, India was the world's only source of diamonds and home to lavish royal courts with jewel-encrusted thrones and palaces brimming with gold and vast treasures. Tavernier was invited to banquets by moguls, whose empires covered much of India. The explorer was stunned by the riches he saw.

On his travels, a coveted blue diamond was often spoken about in hushed tones. Tavernier could only obtain vague information about it. No one was prepared to reveal the secrets surrounding the rarest of gems. Its possessor was said to be reluctant to disclose the history or the whereabouts of the fabled stone. The blue diamond was a stone Tavernier dreamed about. The search led to Golconda.

It was nightfall when Tavernier arrived at the city gates. On the outskirts of the fortress of Golconda, narrow lanes curved around like the tusks of the elephants that swung their tinkling silver bells and chains. Tavernier rested there overnight before travelling for another seven days over plains infested with snakes. His destination, between the Krishna

*Jean-Baptist Tavernier by Nicolas de Largillière, 1678.*

National Portrait Gallery, London.

River and crescent-shaped mountains, was Kollur where the finest diamonds were mined.

Under the watchful eye of overseers, exhausted miners dug pits through layers of gravel that produced a steady revenue. The baskets full of dirt they carted contained some of the largest and most beautiful diamonds ever discovered.

Even with guards to prevent theft, miners, managers and merchants found ingenious ways of smuggling diamonds out of the mines to sell on the open market. Along the alleyways near the Golconda fort, the trade of ill-gotten diamonds was conducted in secret. Vast sums of money exchanged hands.

After lawfully purchasing a rich haul of diamonds from Kollur and nearby mines, Tavernier returned to Golconda. Some believe it was here that he acquired the largest and rarest diamond in his collection. According to legend, a wheezing wretch approached the merchant as he made his way along dusty tracks lined with beggars. At first, Tavernier brushed the man away. Then, from beneath his tattered headcloth, the temple thief fumbled through the greasy coils of his hair. He plucked out a scrap of calico and mumbled into his beard as he undid a knot. Into Tavernier's hand he placed the contents — the luminous blue diamond that was once the sacred idol's eye.

Tavernier's heart raced. Nothing compared to the blue diamond. *It was shaped like a kite*, Tavernier thought, *triangular and crudely cut*. The gem was unparalleled in colour, size and brilliance — the most exquisite diamond he'd ever seen.

'*Un beau violet*,' he proclaimed, admiring the colour. Holding it to the afternoon sunlight, he rotated the stone, examining it for imperfections. It was as clear as water, devoid of speck or flaw, blemish or inclusion. 'Is it yours to sell?' he asked.

The wretch nodded.

'What is your price?' Tavernier asked.

The temple thief batted away the flies. His eyes darted about.

'Let us go somewhere more private,' Tavernier suggested.

For two hours, buyer and seller sat cross-legged under the shade of a tree, haggling back and forth, negotiating the price by hand signals.

*I must have it,* Tavernier thought. The blue diamond haunted him. *But what is a fair value for a stone of such size and rarity?*

The afternoon wore on. The speckled sky burned like fading embers. Finally the wretch uttered an exclamation. A deal was struck. The price remained a secret. 'Leave now,' he whispered as he handed over the precious diamond. Tavernier tucked the misshapen treasure into his leather pouch unaware it would become the most famous gemstone in the world, and ensure his name would echo through the ages.

# FIT FOR A KING

Jean-Baptiste Tavernier took the dangerous sea route back to France via the Cape of Storms in southern Africa. At night, he would retire to his cabin and pour out the contents of his worn leather gem pouch. He counted the glorious diamonds by candlelight and weighed them on his scales.

The unit of weight for diamonds and gemstones is the carat, based on the average weight of a carob seed. At a whopping 112 ½ carats, the blue diamond was by far the largest stone in Tavernier's collection. The ship pitched and rolled and the wind moaned in the sails as he meticulously sketched every detail in his journal, tracing the outline of each diamond's magnificence.

The ship docked in France on a frosty morning in December 1668. Tavernier leaned against the railing. After many months at sea, it was good to be home.

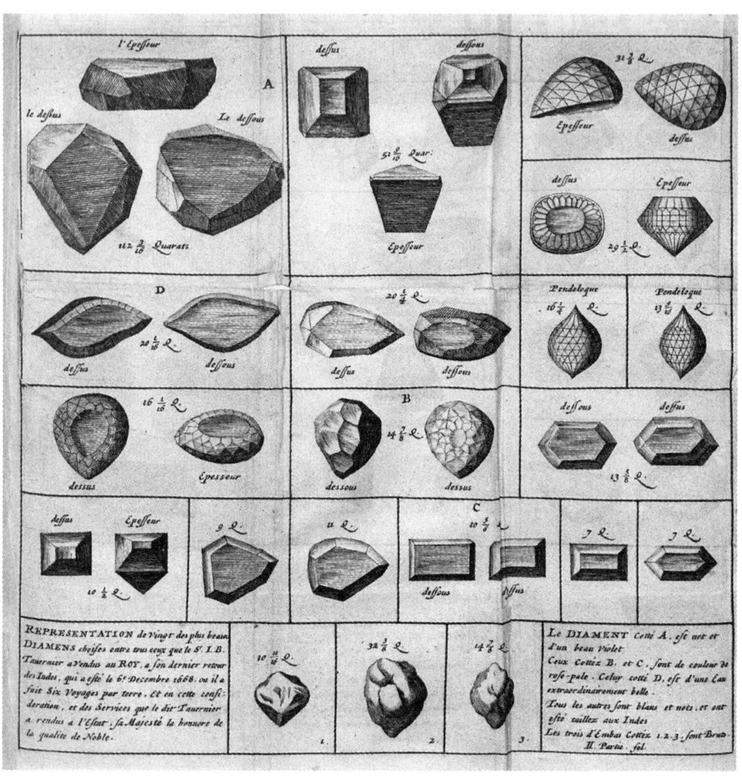


*Diamonds collected by Jean Baptiste Tavernier.*
*The blue diamond is top left.*

He'd undertaken six gruelling voyages from Europe to the Far East. Over the years he'd become an expert in pearls and rare gems. His final journey was devoted to collecting diamonds that he hoped would tempt the king. With his riches safely locked in a strongbox, he climbed aboard a horse-drawn carriage and set off on the overland road to Paris.

In 1668, France was the most powerful nation in Europe, and diamonds were the most cherished item in the royal treasury. King Louis XIV was an avid collector. Known as the Sun King, he literally shone with glittering rings, bracelets, diamond belts and buttons. His sword was encrusted with diamonds. He even had diamonds mounted in the buckles of his shoes. The king dazzled from top to toe and diamonds confirmed his glory.

Louis XIV awaited the arrival of the famous traveller, who had recently returned from India. The king was eager to view treasures from distant mines. Tavernier was honoured with a private audience. He was confident the blue diamond, along with the spectacular collection of other stones, would appeal to the monarch.

Tavernier bowed deeply. After exchanging formal courtesies, he opened a velvet pouch and spread out the glittering contents.

The king gasped upon seeing the blue diamond. He cradled it in his lavender-scented hands.

'You chose well,' noted Tavernier. 'Blue is the rarest colour of all.' Even though nature had formed it misshapen, the diamond was a divine stone, and the colour complemented the king's royal robes.

Louis XIV purchased all Tavernier's diamonds and, in consideration of services to the monarchy, granted the merchant a noble title — Baron of Aubonne.

With his newfound wealth, Tavernier purchased a castle. But after spending the profits from the sale of diamonds too freely and being robbed by a treacherous nephew, he soon found himself financially ruined.

To recoup his losses, Tavernier set off on one last voyage. He travelled to Moscow where, it was said, the adventurer died on the snowbound streets after a pack of wolves surrounded his tent and tore him to shreds. Thus, far away and long ago, the sinister curse of the blue diamond was rumoured to have cast its spell.

Meanwhile, Louis XIV commissioned his court jeweller to reshape the 'French Blue', as it was now known, to give it symmetry, release its fire and maximise its brilliance. To achieve optimum angles and proportions, it was reduced in size from the original French weight of 112.5 carats to just over 67 carats. It took the jeweller nearly two years to cleave and saw, brute and polish the rough stone into a heart-shaped gem the size of a pigeon's egg. Fifty-eight luminous facets snared the light, reflecting rainbow-coloured sparks. The exquisite diamond was set in solid gold and worn by the Sun King on ceremonial occasions.

For a time, Louis XIV lived a happy life. Hunting trips occupied his days, followed by lavish evening parties. At Versailles, in the grandeur of the palace's candlelit Hall of Mirrors, light bounced, leapt and flashed from the diamond's facets. But with the

French Blue pinned to a ribbon on his chest, the king began to slur and stoop. With France fighting costly wars, affairs of the state consumed his days. Some say the wicked intent of an ancient curse was to blame when his toes turned black and shrivelled. Crippled by gout, the king could hardly walk. Worms grew in his stomach and he died as pale as the marble statues surrounding the palace.

For years the blue diamond lay unappreciated in the royal cabinet of curiosities until the new king, Louis XV, discovered it in a rosewood drawer. He admired its colour and fiery splendour. 'Make it into an emblem of chivalry,' he demanded.

With artistic mastery, the royal jeweller created an elaborate pendant — an emblem of the Order of the Golden Fleece. A red spinel was carved into a fire-breathing dragon. Diamonds and sapphires studded its wings. The French Blue was set as the elegant centrepiece that hung from a ribbon that graced the king's chest.

*The French Blue, set in the insignia of the Royal Order of the Golden Fleece.*

But bad luck followed. After surviving a hopeful assassination, red spots appeared on the king's swollen face. He died in agony two weeks later, covered in foul-smelling smallpox scabs.

Following the death of Louis XV, the diamond remained unseen in the darkness of a drawer. The next in line to the throne eventually rescued the blue diamond from obscurity, but the times were changing. After years of war, the treasury was bankrupt. King Louis XVI ignored the rebellious mood of the people that was growing ever more dangerous. The citizens of France rioted when taxes increased. Acts of defiance became common as the people turned against the king and his wife, Queen Marie Antoinette.

For a time, the queen was oblivious to the grievances of once loyal subjects. Although there is no record that she ever wore the blue diamond, she continued to adorn herself with other crown jewels. But trouble was brewing. She could not appear in public without being insulted by foul-mouthed mobs.

Her hands trembled and the jewels, once a sign of majesty, were viewed as vulgar symbols of pomp and privilege. 'Mon Dieu,' Marie Antoinette sobbed, 'what will become of us?'

Hunger and anger fuelled the discontent of starving workers and peasants. The French Revolution began. Insurgents stormed the Bastille, a fortress symbolising royal authority. Blood flowed in the streets. Castles burned to the ground. Church bells summoned citizens to attack the royal palace. Soldiers deserted their posts and the king's troops refused to fight.

The king and his queen crammed the crown jewels, including the blue diamond, into satchels and attempted to flee the city at midnight, but their carriage was stopped after the royals were recognised. The king and queen were escorted back to Paris, guarded by a citizens' militia. 'Off with their heads,' cried the angry mob.

Both the king and queen were charged with treason and condemned to the guillotine. Meanwhile, the crown jewels were taken to a secure storehouse — the

Garde-Meuble. Every day, the symbols of royal excess — artworks and tapestries, suits of armour, sceptres and swords encrusted with jewels — were displayed for the public to see. Diamonds represented everything the citizens of France had come to detest. Pickpockets and petty thieves joined the long queues, viewing the treasures, eyeing the locks and exits.

Calls for tighter security at the royal storehouse were ignored. At the same time, a motley crew of ruffians met each night in a dark tavern. Cadet Guillot was one of the lowlives skulking around. He was a burglar known for slithering his way into the homes of the rich and powerful. 'Gather around,' he said. The scoundrels clinked their glasses and drank a toast.

Something big was brewing.

# CROWN JEWELS

On 11 September 1792, the moon was waning and gloomy. Paris was a dangerous place to be after dark. Rogues and scoundrels lurked in the shadows.

Inside the poorly guarded storehouse, royal treasures were packed in boxes and locked in cabinets. The doors on each floor were sealed with wax so break-ins could be easily detected. But even after security for the nation's treasures was questioned, guards often arrived late or failed to turn up at all, leaving priceless jewels and valuables vulnerable.

At 11.00 pm that dark September night, a group of thieves gathered in front of the storehouse building. The ringleader, Cadet Guillot, tossed up a weighted rope and hooked it over a lantern. One by one, six agile robbers shimmied up the rope and climbed over the first-floor balustrade. They broke a windowpane and reached inside to release the catch. The great heist of the French crown jewels was underway.

By candlelight, the robbers pried the locks off cabinets and helped themselves to as many precious objects as they could carry. Cadet Guillot opened a glass-topped walnut case and couldn't believe his eyes. He snatched a jewel-encrusted insignia with a dazzling blue diamond as its centrepiece. While the others grabbed as many jewels as possible, Cadet Guillot slipped the Order of the Golden Fleece into his grubby pocket and shimmied down the rope.

The following day, guards inspected the unbroken wax seal on the outside of the door. Satisfied that no one had broken in, they assumed the crown jewels were safe. 'Nothing to worry about,' they reported to their superiors. Over the next few nights, a bigger band of villains returned and helped themselves to jewel-encrusted swords, diamond chains and other famous Golconda diamonds. On the night of 17 September, a passing group of national guards arrived just in time to capture the last two thieves as they clambered down the rope. By the time the theft was detected, it was too late — the royal collection had been plundered.

During the looting spree almost all the crown jewels were taken, including nine thousand gems. Many of the stolen items were later recovered. Some of the diamonds were found buried under a tree. Other national treasures were hidden in attics and scattered at various locations around Paris.

But the blue diamond was gone, and so was Cadet Guillot. Realising the Order of the Golden Fleece was far too recognisable and would be difficult to sell in France, he smuggled the emblem of chivalry out of the country. On route by fishing boat across the English Channel, he pried the blue diamond from its setting and cradled it in his clammy hands.

For twenty years, from 1792 to 1812, the French Blue's whereabouts remained cloaked in mystery. It was rumoured Cadet Guillot sold the diamond for a fraction of its value before he vanished down a dark alley in London's murky underworld, never to be seen again. The diamond was then peddled through London's pea soup fog by a chain of shadowy dealers attempting to snare a buyer.

Diamond merchants pride themselves on knowing the background of valuable stones and the chain of ownership. And the French Blue was no ordinary gem. To disguise the stolen diamond, its shape was altered, reducing its weight from 67.5 carats to 44.5 carats. The treasured gem had drastically shrunk in size from when it was the prized jewel of three French kings. It was now a fraction of the original weight it was when Tavernier brought it back from India. It was rumoured that the jeweller who recut the stone became another victim of the curse after he died a ruined man.

In 1812, just two days after the twenty-year statute of limitations expired for crimes committed during the French Revolution, a curious and extremely rare blue diamond was offered for sale. With the threat of prosecution for theft now eliminated, the owner was comfortable advertising a 44.5 carat blue diamond of

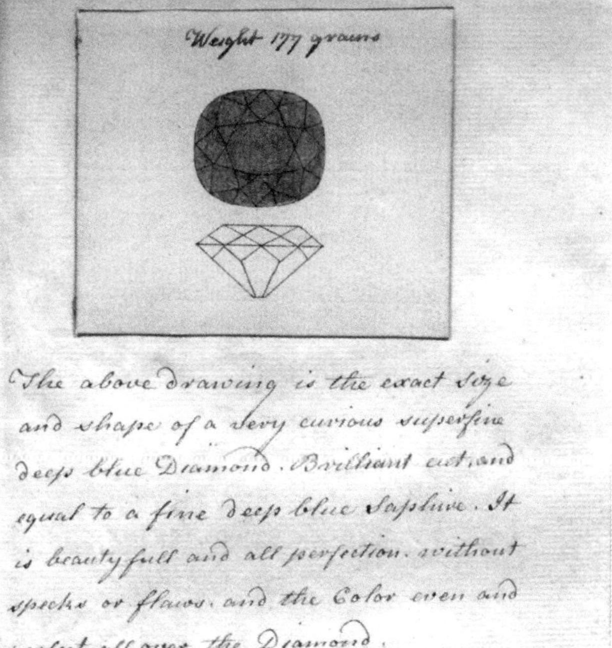

Weight 177 grains

The above drawing is the exact size
and shape of a very curious superfine
deep blue Diamond. Brilliant cut and
equal to a fine deep blue Saphire. It
is beautyfull and all perfection. without
specks or flaws. and the Color even and
perfect all over the Diamond.
I traced it round the Diamond with a
Pencil, by leave of Mr. Daniel Eliason and it is as finely cut as I have
ever seen a Diamond.
The color of the Drawing is as near the color
of the Diamond as possible. John Francillon
19th Sept 1812 No. 24 Norfolk street
Strand London

*1812 description by London jeweller, John Francillon. The earliest record of what would become known as the Hope Diamond.*

U.S. Geological Survey Library.

beauty and perfection. The history of who owned it and where it came from was not mentioned.

The ruler of England, George IV, was fond of diamonds and precious gemstones. 'I must have it,' he insisted. Although no written evidence exists linking him to the French Blue, it is believed that an unrivalled blue diamond ended up in his possession.

After adding the diamond to his collection, the king's health declined. His eyesight failed and he died grotesquely bloated and plagued by gout after feasting and drinking. The blue diamond was secretly sold to pay off the king's debts. Its next owner would give it the name it would be known by forever.

# HOPE

Henry Hope christened the diamond with his family name — the Hope Diamond.

'It's a gem of extraordinary perfection,' he boasted. The new owner was a wealthy collector of pearls and precious stones. He kept his treasures, which included over forty coloured diamonds, in a large cabinet with sixteen drawers. Pride of place was given to the superfine deep-blue diamond, mounted in a medallion with small rose and colourless diamonds surrounding it.

Henry Hope often retired to his study and opened drawer number sixteen. He stared into the diamond's heart, examining its charming sparks of light. He picked up a quill pen, dipped it in ink, and searched for the words to describe its splendour:

*It is a matchless gem that combines the colour of*

*the sapphire with the prismatic fire and brilliancy of the diamond. There exists no cabinet in the world that can boast possession of a gem that compares with this blue brilliant.*

With the diamond in his possession, Henry Hope grew lonely and frail. As the years passed, his mind became befuddled. His greatest fear was that he would lose his senses altogether. Hunched over his desk, he cradled the blue diamond. *What will happen to you after I'm gone?* he wondered.

Following his death, the family traded insults over who would inherit the valuable collection. Lawsuits dragged on for years. While lawyers grew rich, the legendary jinxed jewel was kept in the dark, languishing in a bank vault. But a diamond needs light and adoring eyes.

The family finally agreed to display the heirloom at Queen Victoria's Great Exhibition in 1851. Lying on white satin, the famous blue diamond enchanted millions of people. After the exhibition, it was returned to the bank vault for another five years before being

*Henry Philip Hope by Thomas Goff Lupton, 1823.*

National Portrait Gallery, London

sent to France for an exhibition in Paris. Millions of awestruck faces filed past, unaware that the main attraction was once one of the stolen French crown jewels.

Henry Hope's grandson, Lord Francis Hope, eventually inherited the blue diamond. But the debonair aristocrat lived extravagantly, squandering his fortune. After gambling his money away, he shot himself in the foot while hunting. In 1901, Lord Francis offered the Hope Diamond for sale to avoid bankruptcy and to rid himself of the 'bad luck' stone.

A London diamond dealer purchased it and promptly sold it to a New York jeweller who, in turn, sold it to a collector who acquired it on behalf of the Sultan of Turkey, who sold the hoodoo diamond after facing financial ruin. At auction, the diamond passed from one owner to the next until it came into the possession of a smooth-talking Frenchman, experienced in the art of concocting wild stories to inflate the price of precious jewels.

And Pierre Cartier had a story to tell.

# UNLUCKY CHARM

The savvy jeweller swaggered into a gilded hotel lobby. Pierre Cartier was dressed to impress in a silk hat, oyster-coloured spats and knife-edged trousers. He tenderly carried a package sealed with wax. He had in his possession a rare diamond and a fascinating story to tempt a wealthy customer. Embellishing a gemstone's history helped seal a deal and gave the buyer an exciting tale to recount to admirers.

The suave salesman was as polished and flashy as the diamond he intended to sell. He bowed and delicately kissed the hand of the wealthy heiress, Evalyn Walsh McLean. Her father was a penniless Irish immigrant who tried his luck gold prospecting and struck it rich. Evalyn married Edward 'Ned' McLean, the heir to the *Washington Post* newspaper fortune. It was widely reported the newlywed couple had more money than sense. Previously, Evalyn had purchased the Star of the East, a 94.8-carat pear-shaped diamond. 'I cannot help myself,' she admitted to Cartier. 'Shiny rocks make me happy.'

'If you will permit me,' Cartier said, tapping his polished fingernails on the mysterious package. 'I have here the most beautiful gem in all the world. Once, it was the blue diamond of the French crown. More recently it is known as the Hope Diamond.'

Evalyn was instantly interested. 'I must confess,' Cartier continued, 'some believe the diamond is cursed.

'Tell me more,' Evalyn asked the smooth-talking Frenchman.

'References to a curse can be found in a recent article in the *London Times*,' Cartier said. He recounted the story, adding his own savvy sales pitch. 'A gem merchant named Tavernier brought it back from India and sold it to the King of France. After his death, other French kings owned it. Queen Marie Antoinette wore it, so I understand.' Cartier sighed.

'She was guillotined, along with her husband, Louis XVI. The French Blue, as the diamond was known at the time, was stolen during the revolution.'

'A most entertaining tale, Mr Cartier,' Evalyn said. She was eager to see the curious treasure sealed up in the package. But the slick salesman did not open it. Instead, he continued tracing out the jewel's sinister history. 'One might be excused for believing the many misfortunes were the result of a curse. How the gem merchant Tavernier acquired the diamond remains a mystery. Perhaps he was aware it was the stolen eye of an idol,' Cartier said. 'After he sold the diamond to the King of France, Tavernier was torn to pieces by a pack of wolves.'

Evalyn was impatient. 'Let me see the thing.' She could wait no longer.

The Frenchman breathed in quietly. His pause was eloquent. 'No other gem I know of is so rare,' he said. Slowly, delicately, Pierre Cartier peeled away layers of wrapping to reveal the blue diamond.

Evalyn gasped. *The jewel stares at me,* she thought.

The bewitching diamond made her dizzy. The colour puzzled her. *Peking blue would be too dark*, she thought. *Steel blue? Harbour blue?* Each time she turned the jewel, the colour changed. *Blue as a kingfisher's wing*, she thought. No words seemed to adequately describe its magnificence. Framed by a flattering circlet of smaller colourless diamonds, a platinum chain completed the exquisite necklace.

As Evalyn gazed at the jewel, Cartier told her things he could not vouch for — that it would bring bad luck to anyone who possessed it and that the curse could be traced to the idol's wrath. 'Nonsense,' Evalyn snapped. She hung the chain around her neck. 'Bad luck objects are lucky charms for me.'

'Ah, yes madame,' Cartier said. 'The blue diamond looks magnificent. The superstitions we speak of are baseless. Yet, one must admit, they are amusing.'

Evalyn Walsh McLean had fallen under the diamond's spell. 'I simply must have it.'

Her husband, Ned, looked up over his newspaper. 'How much?' he asked.

*Washington socialite Evalyn Walsh McLean wearing the Hope Diamond.*

Getty Images.

The price for the Hope Diamond was the equivalent of nearly US$6 million today. The contract included a clause stating that should extreme misfortune occur to the family within six months, the diamond could be exchanged for jewellery of equal value.

As soon as it became known that Evalyn was the new owner of the infamous Hope Diamond, she received letters from strangers begging her to get rid of the cursed object. Sensationalist headlines and reports about the 'sinister jewel' mixed rumour and myth as fact, which fed a growing source of misinformation. For many readers, the disasters associated with it were believable. Evalyn was fascinated by the diamond's dark history, but not concerned. 'I don't believe in silly superstitions,' she told her friends. 'But I must confess, this thing has got me nervous.'

To ease her worries, Evalyn decided to have a priest bless the stone. Monsignor Russell donned his robes and placed the diamond on a velvet cushion. In a small side room of the church, the priest began his preparations just as a storm broke. No wind. No rain. Just a sudden gloominess with vivid flashes of lightning that struck a tree across the street. Claps of thunder shook the church. The priest's blessing gave Evalyn comfort, and for the rest of her life Evalyn Walsh McLean wore the Hope Diamond as a lucky charm. She was rarely seen in public without it.

Evalyn loved the diamond's notoriety and never missed an opportunity to flaunt it. She even wore it swimming. At home, she hid it inside couch cushions or in her toaster or clock. Mike, her Great Dane, sometimes wore it on his collar to amuse friends at lavish parties. Ambassadors, dignitaries, politicians and world leaders were on her guest list. Evalyn's favourite party game was to hide the famous diamond and then insist visitors 'find the Hope'.

The dazzling diamond was a symbol of wealth and status. When Evalyn wore it, all eyes were on her. But after she acquired it, her life was beset with tragedy. The family endured kidnap threats. Slowly, her husband's newspaper fortune vanished. After the *Washington Post* was declared bankrupt, Evalyn's

Who Will Next Own this $180,000 Death Jewel
Can Purchaser Be Found For The HOPE DIAMOND, Which Has Come To Be Known as The GEM of Disaster and whose Malignant Rays Are Said to Carry Sorrow and Misfortune to its Owners
Baneful Trail "Red With Blood and Wet With Tears" Ever Since It Was Stolen From India.
Disaster Has Pursued Every Possessor of the Gem, Which "Should Be Thrown Into Sea," She Says.
DARK TRAIL OF THE FAMOUS DIAMOND.
Jean Baptiste Tavernier—Torn to pieces by wild dogs while hunting.
Mme. De Montespan—Supplanted by her rival.
Nicholas Fouquet—Beheaded.
Marie Antoinette—Guillotined.
Princess de Lamballe—Stoned to death.
J. R. M'LEAN'S SON BUYS HOPE DIAMOND
$300,000 for Jewel Owned by Louis XVI. and Worn by Marie Antoinette and May Yohe.
WAS ALSO ABDUL HAMID
Blue Stone, Once of 112 Carats, Credited with Bringing Ill-Luck to Its Possessors.
Special to The New York Times.
Hope Diamond
The Startling History of This Fascinating Stone, the "Curse" That Has Followed It for Fourteen Centuries and the Story of the Ruined Life of May Yohe, Who Once Owned and Wore It
HOPE DIAMOND'S OWNER LOS
Famous Unlucky Stone Also Said to Have Gone Down with the Seyne.
Special Cable to THE NEW YORK TIMES.
HOPE
Sultan
PARIS
newspaper story screams about
THE HOPE DIAMOND CURSE.
The Most Sinister Jewel in His
For 400 years this famous diamond has w
its sinister influence on the lives of those w
The most exciting and vivid sto

ant in Whose Blue Depths Evil Power Lu

mond Mystery

AMOND AGAIN

ED FOR SALE

to be Only $150,000,
t Once Was Bought
r $400,000.

ME TO AMERIC

Buyers Inspect It in
tone Has a Remark-
able History.

e to THE NEW YORK
Oct. 29.—After
pwreck the fan
e largest and m
diamond in the
the open market
spected in London
prospective

M'LEANS DIDN'T KNOW
HOPE DIAMOND TALE

Couple Unaware That
Had Brought

OF DEADLY HOODOO
RRIED BY THE FAMOUS HOPE DIA

aneful influence and then cast it into
the bottom of the sea.
The immense blue diamond
was formerly

revolution, when it was bou
grandfather of

HOPE DIAMOND WORN
AT M'LEAN DINNER

Famous Gem Seen for the First
Time in Public Since It
Changed Owners.

NOTABLE GATHERING

Guests Members of Diplomatic Corps
Entertained by Metropolitan
Singers.

HOPE DIAMOND COMING HE

The Famous Blue Stone Bought b
New Yorker—Price Said to
be $250,000.

LONDON, Nov. 13.—The report tha
famous Hope blue diamond is going to
York is correct. It is in the possessio
member of a New York firm now
way to America from London. Th
loom was sold by order of the Ma
ncery.

is said that the price paid for
nd was $250,000.

If the Hope diamond has been
50,000, as reported, it has prov
ore valuable than has hitherto b
osed, as the outside estimate pla
was £25,000. The gem belonged
Francis Pelham Clinton Hope,
only allowed to sell it after a
fight.

It is not the size of the stone w
it its value, but the fact that it
very large blue diamond known.
karats, while the next larges
Brunswick stone,

IAMONI
Y"
EXAMINER

MOND IS SOLD.

Have Paid $400,000 for
mous Gem.

—The famous Hope dia-
owned by the Joseph
ny of New York,
t is reported, for
ed to have been
f Turkey.

ire blue diamond,
nd it is named in
gems. It was first
ker, Henry Thom-
A larger stone of
in the list of fa-
own as the Tav-

nine-year-old son, Vinson, was run over by a car and killed. Her daughter died of an accidental overdose at twenty-five. Her husband, Ned, was committed to a mental health facility. Evalyn squandered money until debt forced her to sell some of her valuables.

*What might have occurred if I'd never seen or touched the diamond,* Evalyn often wondered, but she had grown dependent on it for charisma. It gave her confidence when she wore it. 'I'm not afraid,' she assured her friends. Evalyn couldn't bear to part with the bewitching blue diamond. It was under her pillow when she gasped her last breath.

Evalyn Walsh McLean and her family suffered a mysterious run of bad luck, but was the curse of the Hope Diamond the cause? Is the misfortune associated with the blue diamond simply a story to sell newspapers or a hoax concocted by a suave jeweller?

# NATIONAL TREASURE

After her death, the court ordered the sale of Evalyn's jewellery to pay off her debts. The Hope Diamond was part of a valuable collection purchased by Harry Winston, the 'King of Diamonds'. Winston was a shrewd diamond dealer dedicated to large and famous stones. In the magnificence of his New York office, he examined the exquisite collection he had acquired from Evalyn's estate.

Winston's reputation was such that his insurance company discouraged photographs and public appearances for fear of kidnapping and ransom demands. His clients included princes, princesses, lords, sheikhs, shipping magnates and billionaires. Armed guards stood watch at doors controlled by electronic locks. The elegant building he worked in was protected by alarms that could instantly summon detectives and police cars that prowled the streets outside.

Harry Winston was a diamond connoisseur. He cradled the blue gem in his hand, rubbed it lightly with a soft cloth and examined it with his loupe. He did not believe in curses, although he noted the Hope Diamond was particularly cold to touch. He searched for a way to describe its colour — twilight blue, moody indigo?

For a time, the famous blue diamond formed part of Harry Winston's 'Court of Jewels', a travelling exhibition that raised money for charity and featured other large and famous diamonds. 'I want to educate the public,' he said, 'to learn more about these stellar stones.'

However, even for an experienced diamond expert like Harry Winston, something about the Hope Diamond made him uncomfortable. He wasn't superstitious, but he was keen to avoid any unwanted calamity. He needed a way to dispose of the gem. The answer came in a flash of inspiration.

Harry Winston believed that America deserved a national collection of gems that could rival the crown jewels of European nations. What better way to start an educational collection than by donating the most infamous diamond in the world? He was convinced that a drawcard like the Hope Diamond would inspire other collectors to donate other jewels and mineral specimens. And the valuation of the Hope Diamond donation could be used as a tax credit.

On 7 November 1958, Harry Winston held the blue diamond one last time. He dropped it into a plain brown envelope and posted it by registered mail to the Smithsonian Institution in Washington, DC. 'If you can't trust the mail,' Harry said, 'who can you trust?'

Delivery of the precious package was entrusted to postman James Todd. Clutching the envelope, he marched up the museum steps, smiling nervously for reporters as cameras flashed. The curse-ridden object was blamed when the postman broke his leg and his house burned to the ground.

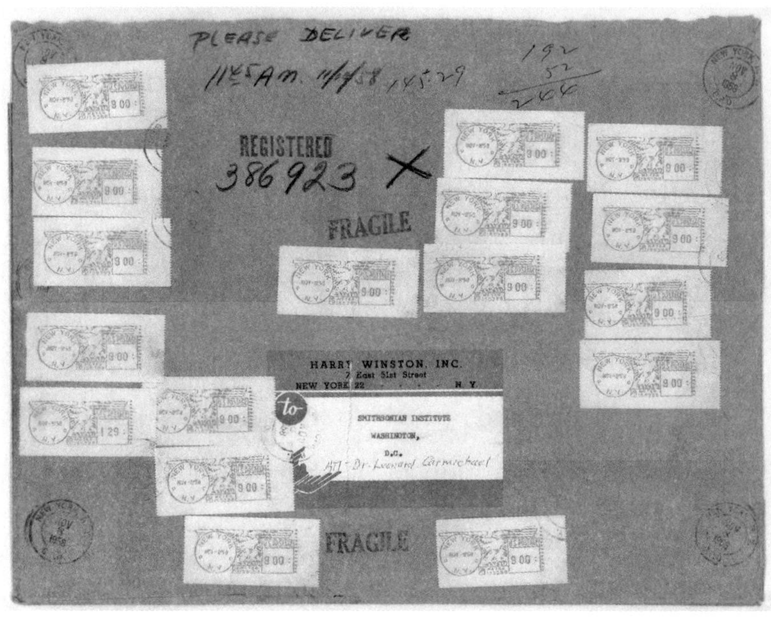


*Envelope that contained the Hope Diamond.*

National Postal Museum, Smithsonian Institution.

Today, visitors from many countries and cultures are drawn to the Smithsonian Museum to gaze upon the showstopper. Enchanted by the mystery and reputation of the world's most notorious diamond, they approach the bulletproof glass pedestal.

The Hope Diamond is dark, greyish-blue, yet every facet sparks and flashes with a rainbow-coloured hue. The colour that gives the diamond its iconic appearance is a result of traces of the element boron, which changes the crystal structure. Such diamonds (classified as type IIb) are semiconductors of electricity. Under ultraviolet light, blue diamonds typically phosphoresce greenish-blue for some time, indicating the slow release of energy.

But there is one notable exception.

When the museum doors close, in the darkness and silence that echoes with the memory of times past, the ancient stone's power becomes visible under ultraviolet light. Mysteriously, the blue diamond emits a blood-red phosphorescence that glows like the molten magma it was born in, the blood of a revolution and the fire-breathing dragon in the Order of the Golden Fleece. These moments in its life colour the diamond, adding another layer of wonder to a miracle of nature that literally 'glows in the dark'.

# ROCK STARS

The ancient fort at Golconda, where great diamonds of the world were traded, now lies in ruins near the modern Indian metropolis of Hyderabad. Another victim of the curse?

Today, Golconda diamonds are still sought after and highly valued for their exceptional transparency, described by experts as pure as ice from a mountain stream, with the luminosity of stars on a cold winter's night. Through the ages, these dazzling gems passed from one owner to the next as the fortunes of dynasties and empires rose and fell.

Like the Hope, many other celebrated Indian diamonds are cloaked in mystery and superstition. Legends conjure a time when diamonds that illuminated temple idols were cursed after being stolen. Stories of skulduggery were not limited to Tavernier's blue diamond. Narratives of other bewitching Indian gems include the Koh-i-Noor or Mountain of Light, a massive stone confiscated by the British from its owners in 1849. It now decorates the crown of the Queen Mother and is preserved in the Tower of London with England's crown jewels. When the Koh-i-Noor came into possession of Queen Victoria, she took the old Indian legends seriously — it was said that the diamond brought misfortune to men who possessed it. Consequently, she specified that it could only be mounted on a crown worn by a woman.

The colonial legacy of looting and the rightful ownership of ancient treasures and cultural property is a topic currently under vigorous debate. Some believe curses were conceived as moral revenge or supernatural retribution for the pillaging and profiteering of sacred objects. Demand is growing for the return of artifacts.

Other Indian diamonds with intriguing histories include the Orloff, a massive diamond of stunning brilliance mounted on the imperial sceptre of Russia.

The Darya-i-Noor or Sea of Light, a large flawless pink diamond, one of the crown jewels of Iran, and 'The Idol's Eye', also have curious histories. The Regent, another Golconda diamond, ended up mounted on the sword of Napoleon Bonaparte and was also one of the jewels stolen from the royal storehouse during the French Revolution.

But among them all, the Hope Diamond is a celebrity gemstone and the most viewed diamond in the world. Each year, visitors shuffle into the Hall of Geology, Gems and Minerals to view a stone of breathtaking rarity and history. 'How much is it worth?' many ask.

Diamonds come in almost every colour, but the subtle changing colours of the Hope — from steel blue to violet to the azure colour of the sea, occurs in only one out of every several hundred thousand diamonds. The money required to purchase even a tiny blue diamond is enormous. Some have fetched tens of millions of dollars at auction. While a significant

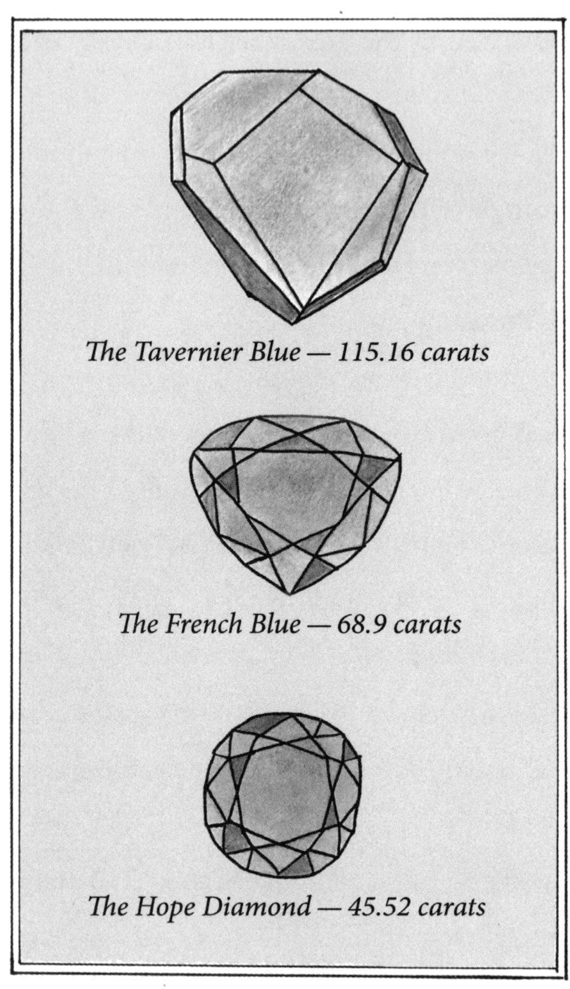


*The transformation in shape and size of the deadly diamond over the centuries.*

portion of a diamond's value is based on the four 'Cs' (colour, clarity, cut and carat weight), other factors, such as rarity and the fame bestowed upon it by human imagination can substantially increase the value.

In 1958, Harry Winston insured the Hope Diamond for one million dollars when he sent it via the post. Today, it is estimated to be worth $US250–350 million. According to the Smithsonian Institute, the Hope Diamond is priceless. Its size, colour and history make it one of the world's great treasures.

A hundred years ago, the elegant salesman Pierre Cartier recognised a fascinating story was just as crucial to a sale as the tastes and financial means of the buyer. Was the story he told about the curse that overwhelmed all who owned the mysterious diamond true? Or was it nothing more than a sales pitch concocted by a newspaper reporter and enhanced by a suave French jeweller?

The sensational newspaper article in 1909 confused ancient beliefs from India and exaggerated the lore of the 'jinxed' diamond. From then on, every published mention of it was framed in the context of its curse. An object worth millions that leaves a trail of death and calamity was good for newspaper sales. But was the public, and Evalyn Walsh, fed a story that had little regard for historical accuracy?

To this day, the deadly diamond retains a spooky reputation as a stone with an ominous sparkle and the power to bring tragedy to anyone who touches it. But does its ownership bring death, dishonour, disgrace or financial ruin? Can the curse of the most famous jewel in the world be reconciled with reality when many of its owners have lived long and generally prosperous lives?

Jean Baptiste Tavernier was regarded as an honest trader. Would he have knowingly purchased a stolen diamond? His tomb can be found in an old cemetery in Moscow. We do know he was 84 years old. Was he devoured by wolves? Or was that a tall tale?

Louis XIV also led a relatively long life, dying four days short of his seventy-fifth birthday. Legends attribute his death to the curse, although he lived for forty-six years after purchasing the blue diamond.

The excruciating pain he suffered was more likely the result of the fast spread of gangrene and the ineffectual medical treatment of the times as prescribed by his physician.

The unrest that preceded the French Revolution had already begun before Louis XVI became king. The curse cannot be blamed for the revolution. While it is true the king and queen met an unpleasant end, according to most researchers, Queen Marie Antoinette never actually wore the blue diamond and probably never even touched it.

The recent discovery of a lead cast of the French Blue at the Muséum National d'Histoire Naturelle in Paris provides experts with evidence that the Hope Diamond was indeed fashioned from the stolen French Blue. Computer modeling based on drawings of the French Blue and a laser scan of both the lead cast and the Hope diamond confirm that the latter was recut from the French Blue. But did George IV, King of England, add a stolen French treasure to his collection? No written evidence exists. If he did own the blue diamond, the purchase and sale were conducted secretly. The price paid and received remains a mystery.

Much has been written about the ill luck associated with those who possessed the diamond, but there is no evidence Henry Philip Hope believed in, or had heard of, a curse. He lived a prosperous life and died without fuss or fanfare aged sixty-five.

The diamond dealer Harry Winston didn't believe in the curse. He kept the diamond for ten years before donating it to the Smithsonian Museum.

Postman James Todd suffered a series of misfortunes within a year of delivering the Hope Diamond to the museum. A truck crushed his leg. His house burned to the ground. But the postman never blamed the curse. 'I don't believe in any of that hoodoo stuff,' he declared.

Today, museum specimen No. 217868 slowly rotates in its bulletproof vault. The deadly diamond has not claimed any new victims. Yet, for many, it is hard to shake off the feeling that there must be some connection between the misfortunes of so many of those who have possessed it.

Each year, museum visitors gaze into the beaming facets of the blue diamond. According to legend, it was once worshipped as the all-seeing eye of a temple idol in ancient India. Now it is seen and adored by millions. Its long history has inspired movies, television series, books and art. And it continues to work its magic. The public do today what worshippers did long ago — they are drawn to the Hope by its mystery.

Round and round it goes, pulsing with energy. Each wink, each ominous sparkle bends light into flashes of colour. Each shift of light reveals a window into the past. The diamond is real, and its history lives on in our imagination. Is it cursed? Or is the legend a cautionary tale?

# THE STORY OF HISTORY

The story of *The Deadly Diamond* took me on an extraordinary journey of discovery. I traveled to India to learn about the gem and diamond trade. I followed in Tavernier's footsteps on the ancient trade route that led me to ruins of the fortress at Golconda and to many other locations connected to the blue diamond. Finally, I visited the Hope Diamond at the Smithsonian National Museum of Natural History in Washington, D.C.

History hunters are intrigued by objects that forge a link with the past — a gold nugget, a relic of war, a shipwreck coin or a cursed blue diamond. These artefacts connect us to history. Each has a tale to tell.

The legendary curse associated with the Hope

Diamond is a mix of mystery and intrigue, fact and fiction. Since it was discovered over four hundred years ago in India, the blue diamond has crossed oceans and continents and implicated a curious cast of characters. The famed Golconda diamond mines in the Deccan plateau, where gem merchant Jean Baptiste Tavernier purchased the miracle of nature, also produced many other storied diamonds — but The Hope Diamond is the rarest and most notorious.

# HOPE DIAMOND STATISTICS

The Hope Diamond is the centrepiece of the National Collection of Geology, Gems and Minerals at the Smithsonian National Museum of Natural History in Washington DC, USA.

The Tavernier Blue — Original weight: 112.5 carats = 115.16 metric carats

The French Blue — Original weight: 67.5 metric carats = 68.9 metric carats

The Hope Diamond — Current weight: 45.52 metric carats

Clarity: VS1 (Very small inclusions not visible to the naked eye)

Colour: Fancy deep greyish blue due to an impurity known as boron.

Cut: Cushion antique brilliant with a faceted girdle and extra facets on the pavilion.

Dimensions:

Length: 25.60 mm
Width: 21.78 mm
Depth: 12.00 mm

*The Hope Diamond is the world's largest-known deep blue diamond.*

Photo © Chip Clark. Smithsonian National Museum of Natural History.

# TIMELINE

Between one and three billion years ago, the blue diamond crystallises 160 kilometers below the earth's surface.

| | |
|---|---|
| 800 BC | Diamonds were first discovered in India. |
| 400 BC | Diamonds were mined in Golconda, India. |
| 327 BC | Alexander the Great introduces Indian diamonds to Europe. |
| 1631 | Jean-Baptiste Tavernier makes the first of six voyages to the Orient. |
| 1642 | A rare blue diamond is discovered in Golconda, India. |
| 1664-68 | Tavernier takes possession of a large blue diamond sometime during his sixth voyage to India. |
| 1668 | Tavernier sells the diamond to King Louis XIV for equivalent US$2.5 million. |

1673 The diamond is recut and named the French Blue.

1689 Tavernier dies in Russia.

1751 The successor to the French crown, Louis XV, has the diamond set into the Order of the Golden Fleece.

1791 June, King Louis XVI and Queen Mary Antoinette are captured attemping to flee France.

1792 On 11 September, the French crown jewels (including the Order of the Golden Fleece) are stolen from the Garde-Meuble. The blue diamond is smuggled by boat from France to England.

1792 In December, King Louis XVI and Queen Mary Antoinette are charged with treason.

1793 King Louis XVI and Queen Mary Antoinette are executed by the guillotine.

1812 A rare blue diamond weighing over 44 carats is offered for sale in England.

1820 The diamond is rumoured to be in possession of George IV, King of England.

1830 Although no record exists of the exact date, it is assumed this was the year that Henry Hope purchased the diamond and it became known as the Hope Diamond.

1851 The Hope Diamond is displayed as part of the Great London Exhibition

| | |
|---|---|
| 1887 | Lord Francis Hope inherits the family heirloom. |
| 1901 | Lord Francis Hope offers the Hope Diamond for sale. |
| 1908 | The Hope Diamond is purchased for the equivalent of $5 million by Selim Habib. |
| 1910 | The blue diamond is in possession of jeweller Pierre Cartier. |
| 1911 | Evalyn Walsh McLean purchases the blue diamond. |
| 1947 | Evalyn Walsh McLean dies. |
| 1949 | Harry Winston purchases Evalyn Walsh's jewellery and diamonds. |
| 1958 | The Hope Diamond is donated to the Smithsonian Museum of Natural History. |
| Today | The Hope Diamond is the most visited object at the Museum, where it slowly rotates on its pedestal, imprisoned by three-inch thick, bulletproof glass. |

# MORE TO EXPLORE

**Books**

Fowler, Marian *Hope: Adventures of a Diamond.* Pocketbooks/Simon & Schuster UK, 2004.

Harlow, George E. *The Nature of Diamonds.* Cambridge University Press, 1998.

Kendall Leo P. *Diamonds: Famous and Fatal.* Robson Books, London 2002.

Khalidi, Omar *Romance of the Golconda Diamonds.* Mapin Publishing, India 1997.

Kurin, Richard *Hope Diamond: The Legendary History of a Cursed Gem.* HarperCollins Publishers & Smithsonian Press, New York, 2006.

Legrand, Jacques *Diamonds: Myth, Magic and Reality.* Crown Publishers, 1980.

Steinem Patch, Susanne *Blue Mystery: The Story of the Hope Diamond.* Random House 1999.

Tavernier, Jean Baptiste *Travels in India.* Macmillan & Co. 1889.

**Weblinks**

si.edu/spotlight/hope-diamond/history

naturaldiamonds.com/rare/the-hope-diamond-the-history-and-science-of-the-priceless-blue-gemstone

thmarch.co.uk/insights/the-hope-diamond-worlds-most-expensive-diamond

naturalhistory.si.edu/history-hope-diamond

# GLOSSARY

Alluvial — sand, soil, gravel, clay and other sediments deposited on land which has been flooded or where a river once flowed.

Boron — rare diamonds get their blue colour from the element boron, contained in the floors of ancient oceans and carried deep into the Earth's mantle by the movement of tectonic plates.

Bastille — a fortress in Paris known as the Bastille Saint-Antoine.

Brahmins — a priestly member of the highest Hindu caste.

Carat — a unit of weight used to measure all gemstones, including diamonds.

Caste — a class in the Hindu system governing social rank.

Curse — an utterance or an object with supernatural power that can inflict harm or punishment on someone or something.

Diamond — a solid form of the element carbon.

Facet — the flat cut and polished surfaces of a gemstone.

Flaw — a speck, a crack, a fissure or an inclusion in a diamond or gemstone.

French Revolution — a period of French political and societal change that began in 1789.

Garde-meuble — the storehouse for French crown jewels.

Gemstone — a mineral crystal that can be used to make jewellery when cut or polished.

Golconda — area where diamonds were mined and the location of a fortress on the western outskirts of Hyderabad, India.

Mogul — a member of the dynasty that ruled northern India from the sixteenth to the mid nineteenth century.

Octahedron — natural crystal shape of a diamond with eight triangular sides that look like two pyramids connected at the base.

Persia — the historic region of southwestern Asia that is now modern Iran.

Phosphorescence — diamonds that belong to a group called type IIB usually look blue. After they absorb UV light, type IIB diamonds glow in the dark for a short time. This afterglow or phosphorescence can range in colour from blue to pink to fiery red.

Water — an old term used to describe the clarity and transparency of a diamond.

# ACKNOWLEDGMENTS

Alex Allan, Cate Sutherland, Frané Lessac, Marcia Wernick, Alok Chordia, Hugh Durey, Tim Scott and Dr Richard Kurin, Smithsonian Distinguished Scholar and Ambassador-at-Large.

Every effort has been made by the author to contact copyright holders and obtain permission to reproduce material in this book.

# THE HISTORY HUNTER

Mark Greenwood is a History Hunter. He enjoys delving into baffling mysteries, searching for lost treasures and investigating unsolved cold cases.

*The Deadly Diamond* took him on an extraordinary journey of discovery. Visiting the places where history happened helps Mark to speculate about how it was to live at that time, so he can give readers an understanding of sometimes complex events.

History is not an exact science. There is so much we simply do not know. Evidence may exist in the form of the surviving remnants of the past — a document, a book, a newspaper, a map, a setting or an artifact. Objects with interesting stories from the past, like the Hope Diamond connect Mark to history. Steeped in legend, they open up a window to the past.

Find out more at about Mark's award-winning books at markgreenwood.com.au

IF YOU LIKED

JOIN
THE HISTORY HUNTER
FOR MORE . . .

MARK GREENWOOD

HISTORY HUNTER

# THE WONDER HORSE
# SAMPLE CHAPTER

In 1929, the US stock market crashed, sending countries worldwide into the Great Depression. The crippling financial catastrophe caused massive social disruption. Unemployment skyrocketed. Hungry people queued for food. In dark times, a hero was needed to lift the spirits of ordinary Australians. The call was answered by an underdog with unflinching courage who refused to be defeated when the rules were stacked against him.

The story of the Wonder Horse involves a web of mysteries, from the intuition of a struggling horse trainer to the baffling puzzle of genetics that transformed an unwanted animal into a champion. At the story's heart is a bond of trust forged between a young man and a magnificent animal.

Ultimately, the greatest mystery revolves around what happened to the people's champion when he was at the peak of his powers. After defeating all rivals in Australia, the beloved horse sailed to the United States to compete in the richest horserace in the world. What occurred there would secure his legendary status and spark one of our nation's most enduring mysteries.

Four years earlier, on a hot afternoon in New Zealand, the last horse in the yearling auction was offered for sale. Lot No. 41 was a lanky fifteen-month-old, foaled in a picturesque paddock in Timaru.

Entering the sale ring, the clumsy chestnut horse with a small white star on his forehead tripped over his long legs. He lacked the poise of the thoroughbreds that had graced the ring earlier that day. Lot 41 wasn't rated highly.

Even a bargain price was unaffordable for a struggling Australian trainer — but Harry Telford had a hunch. Year after year, he'd wasted money on inexpensive horses, hoping to train one that would win a few races and pay the rent. None had turned out any good. Harry was broke, but he never gave up on his dream. He sat up, night after night, in rented Sydney stables, re-reading the crumpled New Zealand sales catalogue. He pencilled a note next to a horse whose breeding he fancied. *There is something special about Lot 41*, he thought.

Intuition or 'gut feeling' is one of life's great mysteries. But is this remarkable phenomenon real? Is it possible that an inner voice guides us? Or was Harry's hunch really informed knowledge? His obsession with Lot 41 was based on the mystery of genetics and a careful study the horse's pedigree chart. Its father (sire), Night Raid, carried the blood of great British stallions and was the great-grandson of the famous Carbine, who'd won the 1890 Melbourne Cup. Entreaty, its New Zealand–bred mother (dam), was a quality black mare descended from a fine pedigree. Although the parents were well-bred, both were underachievers. Their offspring, the ungainly chestnut colt, stumbled as he walked. Harry scrutinised its bloodlines. The further back he went, the more his faith in the animal's potential grew. *This is a perfectly bred horse*, he thought.

Without the money to pay for Lot 41, Harry badgered several trusted horse owners to bankroll the purchase. No one was willing to risk their money on a hunch. Finally, Harry convinced a wealthy American-born businessman, David Davis, to put up the money for the unnamed horse. Harry wrote to his brother in New Zealand with instructions: 'Make a bid for Lot 41 if you can get him under 200 guineas.'

The sweaty stench of horses mingled with dust that hot afternoon in January 1928. At 5 pm, the last horse was led into the sale ring. 'What am I bid for Lot 41?' the auctioneer asked. 'Am I bid 100 guineas?'

Harry's brother raised his hand.

The only other bidder counteroffered at 150 guineas.

'Do I hear 160?'

Harry's brother nodded.

The other bidder remained silent.

'All done?' asked the auctioneer. The hammer fell, and the clumsy colt was sold for a bargain price.

One month later, the nervous young horse arrived in Sydney, Australia, after a rough trip across the Tasman Sea. David Davis, the new owner, was furious when he laid eyes on the creature. It was skinny, with warts and pimples all over its head. 'You call that thing a horse?' he said. 'I don't want it — and I'm not wasting another penny to train it.'

Harry didn't have the money to purchase the horse himself. He solved the impasse by offering to rent him for three years. 'I'll train and feed him,' he said, 'and enter him in a few races.'

'Alright, Harry,' David Davis said. 'I'll lease him to you, and if he ever wins a race, I'll take a third of the prize money.' A handshake sealed the 'gentlemen's agreement'.

Jockeys and stable hands laughed when they saw the long-legged creature in Harry's care. 'Looks like a cross between a kangaroo and a giraffe,' they joked. Harry ignored their jokes. He was a shrewd judge of horses with high hopes for the awkward young colt with no name.

Aubrey Ping, a medical student interested in languages, often took a break from university studies to watch Harry train his new horse in Centennial Park. He suggested naming the horse Far Lap, an anglicised version of a Thai phrase, roughly translated as 'light in the sky' or 'lightning'. Harry liked the name — but he was superstitious. 'Melbourne Cup winners should have a two-word name,' he said, 'with seven letters.'

'No problem,' replied Mr Ping. 'Replace the F with PH.' And so, the horse was christened Phar Lap.

TO FIND OUT MORE, READ

# OTHER MYSTERIES WITH

A lost plane. A missing pilot. Strange sightings.
An extraordinary recorded coversation.

**ARE WE ALONE IN THE UNIVERSE?**

# THE HISTORY HUNTER

Valuable silver coins, ancient treasure chests, obscure objects and an unidentified skeleton on a lonely beach.

**WHAT MYSTERIES ARE YET TO BE REVEALED?**